How to Write:

A Primer

By Barney Beard
1st Edition

Winner
2020
New England Book Festival

Other Books by Barney Beard

Chapter Books

The Bow Window

The Amazing Adventure of Carter and the Pie Rats
New England Book Festival-Award Winner

The Incredible Adventure of the Eight Cousins
FAPA Silver Medal Winner

The Book Visitors
The Strolin' Dolan
The Horrible Word Hole
The Great Alphabet Adventure
Summer of '19
Their New, Big, Old House
Shut Up and Dance
The Ordinary Man and the Book Dragon
Luke and Carter: Their Summer Adventure
Melody and Connor: Christmas with Grammy
Melody and Connor: Their Visit with Grammy
Oliver and Quinn Travel in Space
Luke and Carter's Winter Adventure

Books for Early Reading

Five Little Monkeys
Conner Can Read
Our Favorite Nursery Rhymes
Luke's Great Adventure Begins
Carter Finds His Imagination
Quinn's Great Adventure
Oliver Learns to Read

More Books by Barney

The Old Man and the Book

Where We keep our Indians
Historical Novel

The Ordinary Man: A Poem
New England Book Festival Winner-First Place

Golf for Beginners
Double Award Winner-FAPA Silver & eLit Bronze

Letters to My Grandchildren

My Collected Poems

The Adventures of Bouncy

Letters to My Grandchildren: Volume II

The Official Rules of Canasta

Golf for Beginners: Left Hand Version

How to Write: A Primer
New England Book Festival Winner-First Place

Writer's Journal
Award Winner-eLit Bronze

A White Killing Frost
New England Book Festival Honorable Mention
Historical novel woven around the Cherokee Nation's
deportation from northwest Georgia. 1820-1838

How to Write: A Primer

By Barney Beard - 1st Edition

Winner: 2020 New England Book Festival

Edited by Connie Schultz
Reader: Beth Kalamanka
All Rights Reserved

ISBN:9798699388073

You've always had the power
my dear,

You just had to learn it
for yourself.

The Wizard of Oz – L. Frank Baum

The Writer's Credo

I have one over-riding passion. I want to lead you to a magnificent window of your own mind, the window with the most spectacular view of all. As you stand in amazement, I will know by the look on your face the vista before you will never be forgotten. That will be the moment of my consummate joy.

Barney Beard

You are unique, one of a kind, God's special creation. No one has ever been or ever will be like you. Inside of your mind are visions no one else will ever see, unless you write, of course. Then everyone can see.

Barney Beard

There are only four words needed
for any writer to defeat writer's block,
"Once upon a time…"

Barney Beard

Live in the sunshine,
swim the sea,
drink the wild air.

Ralph Waldo Emerson

Table of Contents

Author's Note

I wrote this little book for my grandchildren. I want to encourage them to write. Even if you're not my grandchild and no longer young, you were once someone's grandchild and you were once young. You can pretend. You can pretend your great grandfather wrote this book just for you.

That should do the trick.

Preface

My Dear Grandchild,

I wish you to grow into a happy, literate adult, reading widely and writing about everything. Writing is fun. Perhaps this little primer will help get you started. I want you to use and enjoy your thinker.

Read books old and new. Read novels and short stories. Read history. Read textbooks. Read biographies. Read magazines. Read the cereal box. Learn to write by reading. See how they do it. Read more. Watch less.

As you read your mind will store a multitude of words, definitions, phrases and figures of speech. Your reading will create a reservoir of words enabling your writing to be understood precisely. Being able to write clearly is a supremely useful skill.

Write anything and everything. The more you write, the more you'll learn about writing.

From the day I learned you were going to be my grandchild, I've been thinking about your literacy and writing. I want your thinker to work just as much as your looker. Read and write more. Watch less.

Well, get busy writing. I can't wait to read what you've written. Send me a copy of everything. I especially like letters written in crayon. I love you dearly.
Your grandfather,

Your grandfather,
Barney
xoxoxoxo

How to Write:
A Primer

Write

Barney Beard

This book is for writers everywhere,
For writers who sit, for writers who stare,

For writers who write in the day or night,
For writers who wish to give words flight.

To see words soar and rise to the sky,
Words dressed with a shiny black tie.

For writers who want to give me a fright,
Or those who write of deeds of a knight,

Whatever you do, I beg, I plead,
There's only one thing I shall need,

I need you to write, I need to know.
What is it that makes you glow?

Give me the chance, give me the time,
Oh Please, I want to see inside your mind.

You're so interesting, you're so smart,
I want to know secrets,
That come from your heart.

So find a pen and sit in a chair,
Write on a wall or the back of a mare.

Write on the sand or a cardboard box,
Write on the top of a smiling ox.

Whatever you do, take pencil in hand,
And be a writer-woman or a writer-man.

You can do it, I know you can,
You alone can think of your plan.

Today or tomorrow or maybe next week,
I'll get a letter, the letter I seek.

You'll tell me a story with words galore,
I'll read the story I've been waiting for.

So write, write, write and write some more.
Don't even bother to go to the store.

Write on the glass, write on the shoe,
Write stories for me and write stories for you.
Write stories for me and write stories for you.

I can't wait until you do.
I can't wait until you do.
xoxoxoxoxo

Can You Write?

Of course you can write, you silly person.

If you can read this,
If you enjoy hearing stories,
If you enjoy telling stories,
If you recall special moments in your life,
YOU CAN WRITE.

Of course you can write something interesting because you are interesting. You're the only you in the world. Others would like to read about you, because you are different from them. You're unique, one of a kind—incomparable.

Children are like snowflakes.
Each is different.
Each is a work of art.
No two are alike. Each has a story to tell.

Why Write?

Reading maketh a full man,
Conference a ready man,
Writing an exact man.
Francis Bacon

We imagine, tell, and listen to stories. We watch plays, TV and dream stories. We talk about our friends and neighbors. We're quite unable to stop our mind's desire. We consume boring stories to satisfy our insatiable human addiction. We must have story like an addict his drugs.

I have never found, in anything outside of the four walls of my study, an enjoyment equal to sitting at my writing desk with a clean page, a new theme, and a mind awake.
Washington Irving

Why should you write?

100 years from now someone can visit your mind and know exactly what you were thinking.

100 years from now your great grandchildren can learn about their great grandfather.

100 years from now you can influence people, especially your family.

100 years from now a part of you will live.

The Human Need for Story

I remember the first time a reader told me my story made him cry. The human desire for story must have a source—even a poor source like me. We humans need stories equally with air, water and food.

We imagine, tell, and listen to stories. We watch plays, TV and dream stories. We talk about our friends and neighbors. We're quite unable to stop our mind's desire. We consume boring stories to satisfy our insatiable human addiction. We must have story like an addict his drugs.

Who Should You Write For?
Write for whom?

Write for yourself. Keep a journal. Write every day at least a little bit. Write about anything you're interested in. Write stories. Write about the world outside your window. Write the crazy things that come into your mind when you use your imagination. Write about what you dreamed last night. Write about your daydreams. Write.

You can always write for your grandchildren and thus please yourself. Writing about those things that come into the secret places of your mind where only you go, those things are worth writing about. Write to please yourself. That's the only way to be successful.

A. A Milne wrote for his son, Christopher Robin.

James Barrie invented Peter Pan to entertain the
Davies children.

I never worry what others think of my work. If my
grandchildren like my writing, I've won the only
literary prize worth having.

If writing itself isn't your reward,
you're in the wrong business.

Begin Writing Today
Learn to Write by Writing

If you want to be a good golfer—play lots of golf.
If you want to be a good cook—do lots of cooking.
If you want to learn to draw—draw.
If you want to learn to write—write.

You can't learn to golf, cook, draw or write by wishing it so. You gotta do it.

Begin writing today. Of course you won't be a polished writer when you first begin, any more than you will be a good sketch artist the first day you begin to draw.

There is one thing for sure. You will never be a good sketch artist unless you begin sketching.

You'll never be a good carpenter if you don't begin working with wood and you'll never be a good writer until you begin to write. Write.

Once you begin to write, you'll learn with every
word.

The best time to plant a tree was 20 years ago.
The second-best time is now.
Chinese Proverb

If I had my life to live over again, I would keep a
journal. I've forgotten so much of myself.

Write about cows, pigs, horses and trees.
Write about whatever you please.
Write about the sand and sea.
Write about you and me.
Write.

Learn by Discovery

Nothing is so well learned,
as that which is discovered.
Socrates

There isn't much more tasteless than being forced to do something you don't want to do.

Nothing is more fun and interesting than doing something you want to do. Write about the things that interest you. Learn about the world you live in.
Write.

When you write about the things you want to write about, you free your creative mind to explore your abilities to your limits. And, to your great joy, you will find there are no limits to learning.
Write.

In the history of the world,
no one has ever reached their limit of learning.
Write.

When you write
you will discover for yourself
how YOU can write.

You are unique, one of a kind.
No one will ever write like you.
No one will ever write the things you have to write.
Write.

Anyone Can Write

Learn words, make sentences,
form paragraphs, add chapters.
By George, you've written a STORY.

A journey of a thousand miles
begins with one step.

You've always had the power my dear,
You just had to learn it for yourself.
The Wizard of Oz – L. Frank Baum

There are only four words needed
for any writer to defeat writer's block,
"Once upon a time…"

Five Things Needed to Write

A good writer needs only 5 things:

1. Paper
2. Pencil
3. Desk
4. Chair
5. Glue.

What's the glue for?

Pour the glue on the chair and sit on it.
Write.

You have to start somewhere,
So why not start at the beginning?
Why not start with what you have?
Build on that.
No one builds muscles the first day at the gym.

No one publishes a first draft.

Everyone writes a first draft.

Good writers edit their first draft.

No one begins with a second or third draft.

All writers begin at the beginning.

No one can edit a blank page.

Begin today.

Write.

Write About Your Interests

Write about the things you know.
Write about the things you have experienced.
Write about the things you know, nothing else.

I'll give you the whole secret to short story writing.
Rule 1: Write stories that please yourself.
Rule 2. There is no rule 2.
O. Henry

No one has success in the things they don't enjoy doing. If they do happen to have success in something they don't like they'll hate their job.

Fill your paper with the breathings of your heart.
William Wordsworth

You want to be a good writer?
Imagine you're on top of a mountain
with your blind friend. Your blind friend asks,
"What do you see?"

Write about things you know. Those things you know may be a bit boring to you because you've known them intimately for a very long time, but they'll be fresh and interesting to others.

You'll write about the things you know with a familiarity that will cause your writing to be easily read. Your manuscript will be interesting and flow.

Read, Become a Better Writer

Do you want to become a better writer?
Then read the writings of those who know how.
Figure out how they do it.

Begin by reading. Read everything.
Read, read, read.
Read good books if you can.
Read the cereal box if you can't.
Read.

Outside of a dog, a book is man's best friend.
Inside of a dog, it's too dark to read.
Mark Twain

Read a book, read it again,
Read a story beginning to end,
I think books are my best friends.

I had far rather my grandchildren take up the habit of reading books than watching television or smoking dumb cigarettes.

A house without books
is like a room without a window.
Horace Mann

No ornament of a house can compare with books.
They are constant company in a room, even when
you are not reading them.
Harriet Beecher Stowe

The wiser a man becomes, the more he will read,
and those who are wisest, read most.
Hans Christian Andersen

Never make fun of someone if they mispronounce a
word. It means they learned it by reading.

A room without books is like a body without a soul.
Cicero

Books under the bed, books on the shelf,
books I wrote all by myself.

Read, Read, Read
Barney Beard

Read, read, read and read some more,
Read on your way to the hardware store,
Read when lying flat on the floor,
Read beautiful words you adore.

Read, read, read and read some more,
Read more books for your encore.
Read big books by Lady Gabor,
Read her books as you go out the door.

Read, read, read and read some more,
Read, read, read, I do implore,
Read when you're riding a carnivore,
Read when traveling to Ecuador.

Read, read, read and read some more.
Read to your big black Labrador,
Read to your favorite matador.

Read, read, read and read some more,
Read when you visit your neighbor next door,
Read him an exciting tale of yore,
Read to the lady from Baltimore.

Read, read, read and read some more,
Read to your children I do implore,
Read to them when they're four,
Read to little ones you adore.

Read, read, read and read some more,
Read to your children and read some more,
Read to them, O please don't ignore,
For very soon they'll be out your door.
xoxoxoxoxo

Fill Your Word Toolbox

Words are tools which build ideas.
Fill your toolbox with words.

Make us see. Let us touch.
Give us to taste. Please let us smell.
Let us hear your exciting, tingly, sensuous tale.

Words are, of course,
the most powerful drug used by mankind.
Rudyard Kipling

The difference between the almost right word
and the right word is the difference between
the lightening bug and lightening.
Mark Twain

You can think words, all different kinds,
You can write stories,
They come from your mind.

One's ability to think is in direct proportion to the words and concepts one has stored in the mind. Few words mean small thoughts. The more words you have at your command the bigger your thoughts.

I like good strong words that mean something.
Louisa May Alcott

My task which I am trying to achieve is by the power of the written word, to make you hear, to make you feel—it is, before all, to make you see. That—and no more, and it is everything.
Joseph Conrad

Words—so innocent and powerless as they are, as standing in a dictionary, how potent for good and evil they become, in the hands of one who knows how to combine them.
Nathaniel Hawthorne

The extent of one's vocabulary is also the extent of that person's ability to think. Few words mean few thoughts.

I read in a book once that a rose by any other name would smell as sweet, but I've never been able to believe it. I don't believe a rose WOULD be as nice if it was called a thistle or a skunk cabbage.
L.M. Montgomery, Anne of Green Gables

Words are everything to a person. If a human doesn't have words to put together inside the mind in order to make sense of the world around them, that person is an animal, and a poor animal indeed. If you don't believe me, ask Helen Keller and Annie Sullivan.

Words are to one's mind like fuel to a space ship. If a person has few words at their command their space ship will never leave earth. If you you're your mind to reach the heights, if you want to think magnificent thoughts, if you want to roam the universe in your mind…you must have words and lots of them.

Writing Tools

Six honest servants taught me all I know.
Their names are:
What, Why, When, How, Where and Who.
Rudyard Kipling

What is an idiom?

I thought I would hit the hay but I didn't want to be an old stick in the mud. I could kill two birds with one stone but it would cost me an arm and a leg. It's a rule of thumb that every cloud has a silver lining. If I play my cards right, I can have the best of both worlds. If you want to let off steam, remember you can't cry over spilt milk. If you want to learn more idioms, drop me a line.

Barney Beard

Fill your house with books.
Fill every cranny, every nook.
Fill your house with wonder everywhere you look.

The Three Laws of Learning

The first Law of Learning: Repitition

The Second Law of Learning: Repitition

The Third Law of Learning: Repitition

If you want to learn to write, take pencil in hand and write. Begin today.

The more you write the better writer you'll become.

Use Your Imagination

The most precious thing children have
is their imagination.
Adults are always trying to rediscover theirs.

Do you want to be a good writer?
Imagine you're with your blind friend
on top of a mountain. Your blind friend asks,
"What do you see?"

You might lose your way, or your wealth.
You might lose your shoes or your health.
Never lose your imagination.

Only in our personal creation of stories is the infinite imagination of the human mind fully released. Spoon fed visual images coming from a single outside source titillate our emotions but do little for our intellect. True creativity comes from within. Read, and grow your own imagination. Create your own images. Create from within.
Write.

It doesn't matter what you've been thinking about. There are so many more things you haven't thinked about yet. Keep thinking. Keep writing.

"They had been around adults all their life. They knew the feeling of cold water being splashed on their grand imagination."
The Incredible Adventure of the Eight Cousins

Making Your Writing Flow

Why scatter stones, rotten limbs and other obstacles in the path to your door? If you do, you'll have no visitors. Why use unnecessary words when you write? If you do, no one will read your work.

At some point in the editing process you'll have to delete a portion your own words, words you created inside your own mind. This must be done for the sake of the readability of the book you wish to create. You can't include everything you have stored inside your head in the pages of every book you write.

I avoid paths where I must walk over broken ground. I avoid uneven sidewalks. I prefer a smooth path where I don't have to watch my step. I avoid books that cause me to lurch and stumble.

Clarity in Writing

Do not write merely to be understood.
Write so you cannot possibly be misunderstood.
Robert Louis Stevenson

The difficulty is not writing, but writing what you mean, not to affect your reader, but to affect him precisely as you wish.
Robert Louis Stevenson

When I say writing, O believe me,
it is rewriting that I have chiefly in mind.
Robert Louis Stevenson

If you put the hay down where the calves can get it,
the cows can get it too.

I notice you use plain, simple language, short words, and brief sentences. That is the way to write English, it is the modern way and the best way. Stick to it; and don't let the fluff and flowers and verbosity creep in.
Mark Twain-in a letter to a 12-year-old boy

Inspiration

There's not much more inspiring to a writer, than waking to an all-day rain after a good night's sleep.

Writing and gardening. They both require great patience and a willingness to work in season.

The sure way to success is writing for your grandchildren. Your audience will at some point read it, and it doesn't matter about the rest.

Punctuation

Don't worry about punctuation. Become a writer. Write. Get your words down on paper. Learning to properly puncture your sentences will come. True, punctuation for the modern reader is important, but no one can learn to correctly place commas and periods on a blank page. Write.

Have no fear, there are myriads upon myriads who will give you advice about commas, periods and quotation marks. Few of them actually write.

I agree with Cormac McCarthy and George Orwell
and a host of others,
"No semicolons".

The first thing about good writing is to write a sentence and a paragraph without any other punctuation save a period at the end of the sentence.

If you find you must use commas, semicolons, ellipsis, hyphens, exclamations, bold type, capital letters, etc. to make yourself understood, your sentences are too complex.

Not everyone wants to wade through swamps and explore trackless jungles.

Give your reader a smooth, clean road. Show the way. Make the journey comfortable and the view exquisite. Write to make it impossible for your reader to get lost in a confusing maze of highways.

The Joy of Writing

Nothing will give you more patience and
inspiration in your writing than gardening.

If you have a garden and a library
you have all you need.
Cicero

Learn to Write Emotions

If you *tell* the reader that Bull Beezley is a brutal-faced, loose-lipped bully, with snake's blood in his veins, the reader's reaction may be, 'Oh, yeah?'

But if you *show* the reader Bull Beezley raking the bloodied flanks of his weary, sweat-encrusted pony with a quirt, or have him booting the protruding ribs of a starved mongrel, the reader believes.

Fred East

If when you write, you never cry,
get angry, grind your teeth,
or visualize as if you were there,
perhaps you're writing about the wrong things?

Make the Reader Smile

Don't tell me the moon is shining.
Show me the glint of light on broken glass.
Anton Chekhov

Never use exclamation points, said F. Scott Fitzgerald. He was right. Write your paragraph so the reader feels the exclamation. If you don't get the reader excited with your words, sentences and paragraphs, you're certainly not going to do it with a tiny exclamation point. Mr. Fitzgerald was right. Using an exclamation point is like laughing at your own joke.

Use all human senses when writing. Don't force your reader to use their imagination. Readers picked up your book because they want to experience YOUR imagination.

Make us see. Let us touch.
Give us to taste. Please let us smell.
Let us hear your exciting, tingly, sensuous tale.
Barney Beard

Editing

Substitute 'damn' every time you're inclined
to write 'very'. Your editor will delete it
and the writing will be just as it should be.
Mark Twain

A successful book is not made of what is in it,
but what is left out of it.
Mark Twain

Writing is easy.
All you have to do is cross out the wrong words.
Mark Twain

I avoid paths where I must walk over broken ground.
I avoid uneven sidewalks. I prefer a smooth path
where I don't have to watch my step. I avoid books
that cause me to lurch and stumble.
Barney Beard

When you're nearly finished, polish, polish, polish.
Imagine the manuscript you've written is a new car.
You'll have to put thirty or forty coats of wax on to
get a proper shine. Polish, polish, polish.

Barney Beard

When your manuscript is almost finished, have
someone sit beside you and read it aloud, someone
who reads well. Listen to the cadence of their
speech. Listen.

As you listen, you'll easily recognize awkward
sentences, incomplete thoughts and scenes that have
been poorly described. When your reader stumbles
over the text, fix it right then while they wait silently
beside you. When you hear something you don't
like, fix it. Make it read smoothly.

When you go through the entire manuscript with
your reader, work on it once again beginning to end
alone and then have your reader read the entire
manuscript to you again.

If you do this, you'll make a great many
improvements and you'll have a great many
compliments on the readability of your completed
manuscript.

There's no other way. Reading your manuscript silently to yourself is inadequate to put on those final coats of polish. You can't read to yourself. No one can do that.

Lastly, when you're finished and you go through your manuscript and think it's perfect, it's time to give it to the professional editor/proofreader who will, without fail, find another double handful of mistakes. It happens every time I write. I go over and over and over and over my manuscript. I think I've got it perfect but it wasn't. I must have that second set of professional eyes to have that pristine, finished product. Trust me on this one.

You CAN read to yourself but that second person catches the uncatched by the first person.

Connie Schultz: my editor
Used by permission

Use the Fewest Words Possible

If you want visitors to come to your house, you won't clutter the path to your door with rubbish, odd sticks, stones, broken boxes and barrels. You'll have a neat, clean and unobstructed path to your door. A tidy path will attract visitors.

Unnecessary words pour over the side of a brimming mind.

Cicero

Distill, purify, refine, filter, condense.
Use the fewest words possible
to say what you want to say.

Use the fewest words to communicate your thoughts. Using the fewest words has a way of bringing out what you want to say clearly. Imagine the city of Pompey buried by Vesuvius. Imagine those patient archaeologists painstakingly removing layers of sediment. That's your job. Remove all unnecessary words.

Never think your readers are interested in an endless amount of trivia. Tell them the story. Get to the point. Let them imagine their own trivia. They'll be far more comfortable furnishing their own house than using your old, worn, unfamiliar furniture.

The most valuable of all talents is that of never using two words when one will do.
Thomas Jefferson

If you would be pungent, be brief
It is with words as with sunbeams,
the more they are condensed, the deeper they burn.
Robert Southey

Thinking

If you come to my house and see me staring out the window for extended periods of time you might think me lazy. I'm not lazy. When I'm staring out the window I'm working. I'm at my best. I'm thinking. No one can write without a lot of time spent staring out the window while thinking.

Staring out the window is a necessary part of every writer's day.

Words on paper, pen and ink,
I love it when I think, think, think.
Barney Beard

Writing is Cinema for the Mind

As everyone knows, good writing is cinema for the mind. A good writer will 'set the stage' inside the reader's head with words instead of props.

A good writer puts images into a reader's mind like a stage hand puts chairs, tables, windows, doors and back drops on a theater's stage to help us understand a play.

It would be difficult to imagine what was happening in a play if it were performed on a bare stage. The audience needs props and backdrops. You see what I mean? Well-chosen words, sentences and paragraphs create pictures in the reader's mind. Reading is cinema for the mind.

Reading is a thousand times better than television. When you watch TV, you're allowed only one picture. When you read, your mind can create a thousand different pictures, maybe ten thousand. TV can't do that. More reading, please.

Remember to tell the reader what color things are and how big or small something is.

Help people see things clearly in their mind when they're reading your stories. Help the reader feel the emotions of your characters.

Write as if telling a story to a blind friend. Pretend your friend who cannot see wants to hear your story. Use words to create pictures in your friend's mind so your blind friend can SEE. You are your friend's eyes. Write as if you and your blind friend were on the mountain top and your friend asks, "What do you see?"

Help your readers feel the emotions of your characters as they read. Don't simply write 'a person was angry'. Tell your reader what happened to that person. Write so your reader can feel your character's anger right along with the character.

Don't simply say 'John was sad' and leave it at that. No, tell about John's life. If you want your reader to understand John's character, tell your reader about the unfortunate things that happened to John so your reader can be sad right along with him, maybe even cry.

You want the reader to feel the character's emotions. That's the kind of thing I mean about clarity in writing. That's what I mean about helping the reader SEE.

Writing should create brilliant pictures inside your reader's head as if your reader were in a gigantic movie theatre with a dozen huge screens all the way around. That just about says it all, doesn't it? Reading should be cinema for the mind.

If you want to be a carpenter, be a carpenter's apprentice. Learn from the person who knows how. Watch him. Study how he does it.

If you want to become a better writer, read lots of books. Learn how they put their stories together. Read.

There's one thing I know for certain. You can write. I know you can. Keep writing.

So, the crux of the matter is…
You can always edit a bad page and make it better.
No one can edit a blank page.

YOU CAN WRITE

THE BEGINNING

(This is the Beginning)
(This isn't the end, certainly not)

Some of the Right Books

Put the hay down where the calves can get it,
and the cows can get it too.

It occurred to me a person interested in reading might also enjoy 'some of the right books' that have fueled my imagination and inspired me to write.

I have one over-riding passion for you. I want to take you to a magnificent window in your mind, the window of your own mind with the most spectacular view of all, a window entirely of your own creation.

As you stand before that marvelous window in amazement, I will know by the look on your face that the breathtaking vista before you will never be forgotten. That will be the moment of my consummate joy.

Barney Beard

A Reading List
Some of the Right Books

Chronicles of Narnia….C.S. Lewis
Peter Pan….James Barrie
James and the Giant Peach….Roald Dahl
Captains Courageous….Rudyard Kipling
Winnie the Pooh….A.A. Milne
Mary Poppins….P.L. Travers
The Bow Window…Barney Beard
The Wizard of OZ…L. Frank Baum
The Phantom Tollbooth…Norton Juster
Charlotte's Web…E.B. White
The Incredible Adventure of the Eight Cousins
The BFG….Roald Dahl
The Jungle Book….Rudyard Kipling
The Giving Tree…Shel Silverstein
Willie Wonka and the Chocolate Factory
Treasure Island….Robert Louis Stevenson
Tom Sawyer….Mark Twain
Rikki-Tikki-Tavi….Rudyard Kipling
How the Grinch Stole Christmas….Dr. Seuss
Mary Poppins Opens the Door….P.L. Travers
Little Women….Louisa May Alcott
The Call of the Wild….Jack London
The Great Alphabet Adventure…Barney Beard

The Hobbit...J.R.R. Tolkien
The Lord of the Rings Trilogy...J.R.R. Tolkien
The Wind in the Willows....Kenneth Grahame
The Secret Garden....Frances Hodgson Burnet
The Velveteen Rabbit...Margery Williams Bianco
Where the Wild Things Are...Maurice Sendak
The Little House Collection...Laura Ingalls Wilder
Peter Rabbit...Beatrix Potter
Just So Stories...Rudyard Kipling
Pinocchio....Carlo Collodi
Heidi...Johanna Spyri
Complete Fairy Tales...Hans Christian Andersen
Pollyanna...Eleanor H. Porter
Mary Poppins Comes Back...P.L.Travers
Pippi Longstocking...Astrid Lindgren
Aesop's Fables.......Aesop
A Christmas Carol...Charles Dickens
Grimm's Fairy Tales...Jacob & Wilhelm Grimm
Black Beauty...Anna Sewell
Huckleberry Finn...Mark Twain
A Little Princess...Frances Hodgson Burnet
The Railway Children....E. Nesbit
White Fang...Jack London
Bambi...Felix Salten
The Sword in the Stone...T.H.White
Watership Down....Richard Adams

The Neverending Story...Michael Ende
The Borrowers...Mary Norton
Jumanji...Chris Van Allsburg
Matilda...Roald Dahl
Rumpelstiltskin...Paul. O. Zelinsky
Swiss Family Robinson...Johann David Wyss
The Incredible Journey...Sheila Burnford
Old Yeller...Fred Gipson
Anne of Green Gables....L.M. Montgomery
The Seven Voyages of Sindbad the Sailor, introduction
by C.S. Forester, New York: Heritage Press

There's a million more just like these,
So turn off the TV, please.
Quit mindless video games.
Drop your phone in a bucket of water.
Get busy reading.

51

2 December 2021

9 798699 388073